LAURE-CINTHIE MONTALANT DAMOREAU
(1801–1863)

CLASSIC BEL CANTO TECHNIQUE

Laure-Cinthie
Damoreau

Paris Conservatoire, 1834–1856

New English Translation and Introduction by
Victor Rangel-Ribeiro

DOVER PUBLICATIONS, INC.
Mineola, New York

Bibliographical Note

This Dover edition, first published in 1997, is an expanded and newly translated republication of *Metodo di Canto / Composto ad uso delle Allieve del Conservatorio di Parigi / de Madama L. C. Damoreau / Traduzione Italiana di P. Casati*, originally published by G. Ricordi & C., Milano, n.d., itself a translation of the original French publication *Méthode de chant*, 1849. Victor Rangel-Ribeiro provided the following materials, specially prepared for this edition: an introduction; an English translation of the text, including an expanded list of contents; editorial footnotes to the author's preface; and two appendixes. Headings throughout have been newly typeset.

International Standard Book Number: 0-486-29984-8

Manufactured in the United States of America
Dover Publications, Inc., 31 East 2nd Street, Mineola, N.Y. 11501

Contents

Six Grand Studies

Six Vocalises on Style

Virtuoso Passages, Cadenzas and Reprises
Meant to Embellish a Piece of Music
(from Mme. Damoreau's repertoire
at the Théâtre des Italiens, the Opéra and the Opéra-Comique)

Appendixes

INTRODUCTION

For the greater part of her career, Laure-Cinthie Damoreau (1801–1863, *née* Montalant) sang a distinctly contemporary repertoire, premiering more than twenty leading roles between 1825 and her retirement from the operatic stage in 1849. Performing under the stage name Cinti-Damoreau, she became celebrated for her remarkable extemporized *fioriture*, a dazzling achievement applauded by Hector Berlioz in the published comment that "we sincerely believe the art of vocalization cannot be extended beyond these limits . . . Each note of this sweet voice is a pearl plucked from the most beautiful of waters."

In 1849 Mme. Damoreau—then on the vocal faculty of the Paris Conservatoire since 1833—presented her *Méthode de Chant* for approval by the school. Citing the method's clarity, good taste, elegant examples and careful attention to detail, a committee of Daniel Auber, Giacomo Meyerbeer, Jacques Halévy, Adolphe Adam and Ambroise Thomas unanimously recommended adoption of the method as a text for Conservatoire classes. Her method proved succinct, providing practical, well-graduated exercises to be practiced under the guidance of an experienced teacher.

A Note on the Device Called
Vibration or *Vibrazione della voce*

Damoreau recommended the judicious use of *vibration*, but without explanation for this well-established practice of her time. In his *Méthode complète de chant*, Op. 40 (1826), the celebrated singing teacher Alexis de Garaudé explained the term as follows, describing, in effect, the second half of a *messa di voce*, applied in this way:

> We call 'vibrating the voice' a method of attacking a note strongly and openly, and then letting it diminish by degrees until it ends as a *pianissimo*. This type of attack is much used in Italian music; its effect is to give the voice all the sonority of which it is capable, and to accent the musical phrase. But it should not be abused, as some singers are wont to do. In song, it should be used principally on a syllable on which the accent falls, on an *appoggiatura*, and on the strong beats of a measure, where a more distinct coloration is called for.

A Note on the Cadenzas

The great 19th-century teachers of the Golden Age of Song—Manuel García, Mathilde Marchesi, Damoreau—all provided their students with examples of *bravura* cadenzas to be interpolated in specific arias from the operatic repertoire. Damoreau's cadenzas in this book are ones she herself performed, ones on which she built an international reputation. In studying a role, she noted which arias the composer had left simple and unadorned, which others he had ornamented. She then bent her considerable skills to developing further the *fioriture* in the elaborated arias; the unadorned arias were left intact.

VICTOR RANGEL-RIBEIRO

Linguist, musician and musicologist, Victor Rangel-Ribeiro is author of *Baroque Music: A Practical Guide for the Performer* (Schirmer Books, NY, 1981); and co-author, with Robert Markel, of *Chamber Music: An International Guide to Works and Their Instrumentation* (Facts on File, NY, 1993).

ADVICE TO MY STUDENTS
AT THE CONSERVATOIRE
ON THE ART OF SINGING

To you, my dear students, I dedicate this method, the fruit of my studies and of my experience; I have combined in it the best principles and the best examples of the art of singing. Hold firmly to the principles, and make certain that you reproduce the examples faithfully: here, in sum, is the secret of good instruction.

If I speak to you of my studies, it is because even at the height of my career I never stopped studying. It is only because of assiduous endeavor and a firm resolve to make some progress each day that I had the great honor of winning and holding public favor. To prove to you how much one gains with so much persistence in learning, I had thought of beginning this book with the story of my life; fearing longwindedness, however, I now limit myself to tracing those events in my career that led to my entry into the Théâtre-Italien, the Opéra, and the Opéra-Comique. Let me assure you that, in speaking of myself, I still have you always in my thoughts.

I was barely thirteen when I was brought before M. Charles-Henri Plantade,[1] a man of spirit, a talented and generous man, whose memory is held dear by those who have loved and cultivated the art of music in France over the past thirty years. Maestro Plantade was assiduous in his teaching, bestowing on me all the care of an excellent teacher and all the tenderness of a father; my voice, which held promise of being flexible, and had as yet not much power, seemed to him to be quite suited to the Italian genre.

With him I studied only the old repertoire; we began with the *Psalms* of Durante, and my teacher allowed me to sing no more than three or four French arias. These were taken from *Montano et Stéphanie*,[2] and *Beniowski*,[3] true models of simplicity, expressiveness, and grace. I cite these examples, dear students, so that you might not think that good singing is only possible after one has learned how to sing difficult music easily. In fact, it is never enough to cope with the notes, or to be able to perform passages of greater or less difficulty; one must color the notes, give them life, and accent them, and this is why it is essential that the artist go beyond the words, and enter into the spirit of the piece or scene that he is going to sing. It is also important that his mien should, so to speak, reveal to listeners the subject and the character of whatever is being sung. Need I add that the articulation and pronunciation should also be flawless? Listen to Ponchard,[4] and you will become aware of just how much is gained in effectiveness when not a single syllable is lost on its way to the audience.

It is much more difficult to sing in French than in Italian, and this is easy to explain. We French do not allow ourselves to snatch a breath in the middle of a word, nor to repeat a syllable, nor to sing *forte* when the situation demands that one sing *piano*. Far from sacrificing the text to the music, we subordinate the music to the words. It is possible, if one studies continuously and dedicates oneself exclusively to this art, to reach a point where the words and the notes are as one, and the singer can actually "speak" the music.

Here, then, dear students, is the gist of almost my entire method: I have always studied, I have studied constantly, listening and thinking about everything that I heard.

When I was fourteen, M. Plantade said to me, "Dear child, you can now do without me. Listen: you have good taste; you will adopt whatever is good in some and avoid what's bad in others." Do not conclude from this advice that one must slavishly imitate either a teacher or a model that one adopts. It is necessary—and this will bear repetition—to take note, through careful listening, of the means by which an artist achieves success; one must identify the art through which he charms, and learn the secret through which he enchants. In this manner one avoids the pitfalls of parody, and can make rapid progress along the road to success.

Before I was quite fifteen, I made my debut in the Théâtre-Italien in the role of Lilla, in *Una Cosa rara*,[5] a role that had become available through the departure of Mme. Fodor.[6] Thanks to my extreme youthfulness, and especially to the advice of my beloved teacher, my success was real. That day, the audience's applause confirmed in its entirety the approbation I had received from M. Plantade; it was the best day of my life. Following this fortunate debut, I had many vexations and much prejudice to overcome. I was French, and that in itself was almost an insult to the Théâtre-Italien! But I was not discouraged, and quickly learned some fifteen or twenty roles. I substituted for all the prima donnas, sometimes on barely a day's notice. In the ardor of my zeal and through my ceaseless studies I kept myself ready for any eventuality. Here, my dear students, it is proper for me to tell you that if you are aiming at the theatre, it is not enough for you to study just the one role that you propose to sing; you must also take the other roles into

---

[1][Charles-Henri Plantade (1764–1839), a noted opera composer, was professor at the Paris Conservatoire in the years 1799–1807, 1815–16 and 1818–28.]

[2][This opera by Henri Montan Berton (1767–1844) was first performed in 1799.]

[3][An opera by François Adrien Boildieu (1775–1834), that premiered in 1800.]

[4][Marie-Sophie Ponchard (1792–1873) sang at the Opéra-Comique from 1818 to 1837. Like Damoreau, she premiered works by Auber, and also by Hérold.]

[5][An opera by Vicente Martin y Soler (1754–1806), with a libretto by Lorenzo da Ponte. It was first produced in Vienna on 17 November 1786, a few months after *Le Nozze di Figaro*, and was at the time more popular than the Mozart opera.]

[6][Josephine Fodor-Mainvielle (1789–1870) had gained international acclaim for her performances of Mozart and Rossini operas. Nine years after the *Cosa Rara* incident, she lost her voice while singing *Semiramide* in its 1825 Paris premiere.]

account, and enter into their spirit. In this manner you will be better able to understand the opera's ethos, and you will have taken a most appropriate step towards shaping and developing your talent. This habit that I had formed turned out to be greatly to my advantage.

Mme. Catalani[7] was scheduled to give a special performance at the Opéra. The general rehearsal was already well under way when it was noticed that the great singer had not yet arrived. At the moment when a *ritornello* introduced the cavatina she was to sing, our manager, M. Barilli, took me by the hand and told the orchestra firmly that I would sing in lieu of our celebrated directress. At first greatly flustered, I soon became very happy because the orchestra applauded me greatly, and this was the first time that I had been conceded that honor. When Mme. Catalani learned of my audacity, or rather of the predicament in which I had let myself be placed, good soul that she was, she thanked me by embracing me.

Shortly after, when I was sixteen, García[8] assigned me an enchanting leading role in his opera, *The Caliph of Baghdad*. Garat,[9] who heard me then, remarked that I sang "insolently well in tune"; alas! I was too young then to understand what he meant. But singing in tune is an attribute for which I have been grateful all my life. Strive to achieve it, my dear students; without good intonation, one cannot please. I know that true intonation cannot be handed to you, but by carefully and slowly studying intervals of every type, with the help of a teacher, one can learn to pitch accurately, even though this may not have been a natural gift.

With Rossini's arrival in France [in 1823] I benefitted from valuable advice from Bordogni,[10] who is now my colleague at this Conservatoire; his good taste is evidenced in the charming vocalises he has given us.

It was shortly after this that an extraordinary performance provided me with the opportunity to sing at the Opéra, in *Le Rossignol*.[11] This being the very first time I would be singing in French before an audience, I was deeply anxious. As the performance was a brilliant success, however, I decided to remain in the grand ambience of the Opéra, where it became apparent that new horizons beckoned. Still, before quitting the Théâtre-Italien, which had become dear to me for many reasons, I decided to undergo an even more demanding test than had been posed by *Le Rossignol*. The Viscount of La Rochefoucald (now Duke of Doudeauville), whose name every artist must remember with gratitude, was at that time in charge of the [Académie des] Beaux-Arts. I asked his permission to sing the role of Amazily in Spontini's *Fernand Cortez*, an exquisite part, full of expressiveness and seemingly not in keeping with the type of genre I had cultivated until then. Amazily's role does

not include even one single *roulade;* one could not sing it any other way than simply and with spirit.

This second challenge proved to be even more favorable to me than the first. I therefore joined the Opéra, with the satisfaction of having obtained the support of so eminent a composer as Spontini, and of as dramatic a singer as Mme. Branchu,[12] for whom he had created that admirable role twenty years earlier. Here begins the second and no less happy stage of my singing career.

In this period I redoubled my studies and my efforts to master the broad and expressive style of the genre known as 'bravura', of runs, embellishments, etc. In order to become adept at all aspects of vocal art, I sang romances as well as canzonets. This last type is difficult beyond belief, because it demands to be spoken rather than sung. From this time on I did not depend on any counsel other than my own, because of the profound study I had made of every genre and of every style.

My repertoire at the Opéra was at first somewhat limited. Since I was unable to vary my own roles as I had previously done, I concentrated on varying the virtuoso passages in the music itself. The audiences were constantly changing, but some true opera lovers attended each and every one of my performances, and I could not add even an unexpected *appoggiatura* to one of their favorite pieces without its being immediately noticed, and enthusiastically applauded. However, I must confess that my musical coquetry was aimed most of all at my beloved orchestra; it is from the orchestra that I received the clearest signals of empathy. These were very precious to me, and a quick approving glance from M. Habeneck[13] touched my heart more deeply than even the plaudits of the people.

This facility in varying virtuoso passages, although it provokes applause, should not be pushed to an extreme; it is important that the ornaments be rhythmic, appropriate to the genre and the tempo of the piece, and always subordinate to the words. Beware always of that torrent of notes, lacking in intelligence, in character, and in color, with which mediocre singers try so hard to charm the public; and do not forget, I repeat, that the embellishments must ever be subordinated to the words, because varying a musical phrase should not involve distorting it or rendering it unrecognizable. This aspect of our art is also a vast field of study, and one event will help illustrate this.

A famous singer had arrived in Paris, and the Duke of Duras, who is now first gentleman of King Charles X's royal bedchamber, and whose patronage extended to all the arts and to all artists, wished to hear her sing a duet. On the day of the concert, the celebrated maestro Paër[14] conducted the morning rehearsal. We agreed on how we would perform the virtuoso passages that abound in the chosen duet, which consists almost entirely of question and answer; I was the one who would be responding. At the evening performance an evil thought seized hold of the wonderful singer, and without warning she sang quite differently all the passages we had agreed upon in the

---

[7][Angelica Catalani (1780–1849), internationally known Italian-born soprano, became the director of the Théâtre-Italien in Paris (1814–17) while she was also singing there. Spontini had been offered the post but had turned it down in her favor.]

[8][Manuel del Pópolo García (1775–1832), a famous tenor and opera composer, was also a much sought-after singing teacher. He taught his son, the baritone Manuel García; and his two daughters, Mme. Malibran (contralto) and Pauline Viardot-García (mezzo-soprano), all of whom gained international renown.]

[9][Pierre-Jean Garat (1762–1823) was a very popular tenor-baritone. He had a three-octave range, and could sing tenor as well as bass. He taught at the Paris Conservatoire from 1796 to 1823.]

[10][Giulio Marco Bordogni (1789–1856), Italian-born tenor, sang at La Scala, and at the Théâtre-Italien in Paris. He became a professor at the Conservatoire in 1820. His voice, like Damoreau's, was small but well-placed.]

[11][Popular opera by Louis-Sébastien Lebrun (1764–1829). Damoreau was fifteen when *Rossignol* premiered, April 23, 1816.]

[12][Alexandrine Caroline Branchu (1780–1850), Haitian by birth, joined the Opéra in 1801, and was named *prima donna* in 1826. At the height of her career she was considered the best dramatic soprano in all of France. She taught at the Conservatoire for several years.]

[13][François-Antoine Habeneck (1781–1849) was principal conductor of the Paris Opéra from 1824 to 1846. Among the premieres he led was that of Rossini's *Guillaume Tell*, starring Damoreau as Mathilde.]

[14][Ferdinando Paër, successful operatic composer, was conductor of the Opéra-Comique, and later of the Théâtre-Italien (1812–1827), where his co-conductor was Rossini. He was appointed conductor of the Royal Chamber Music in 1832.]

morning. Greatly disconcerted at first, I did not falter, and through one of those flashes of inspiration that defy explanation, I answered her phrase for phrase without missing a fraction of a beat, improvising other passages where, I must admit, one could sense some of the vexation I felt at the unexpected turn of events. My courage was rewarded; far from losing the battle, I heard it said from all quarters that the duet had never been better sung, by one part or the other. Reconciliation followed success, and our friendship from that day on was marked by the same harmony that prevailed in our duets.

There's a lesson to be drawn from this episode, my dear students; without the facility I had developed in varying every theme, and, by dint of study, in playing with any and every musical phrase, I should certainly have fared less well with my inspiration; it would all have been over for me in that moment, and my reputation, long well-established, would have fallen victim to malice, right in front of the same public that had been so well-disposed towards me and had grown accustomed to applauding me.

At the end of this method, among the cadenzas that I have selected from my entire triple repertoire, you will find some that will not suit all voices, nor all temperaments; their success depends as much on the intelligence of the performer as it does on the manner in which they are performed. For example, one must be an excellent musician and have great surety of intonation to sing those that modulate. I have included them, not so that you might perform them at any cost against the dictates of your nature and your training, but rather to present you with a variety of formulas, so that later on your own good taste might lead you to devise others that would be better suited to you, within the limitations of your means. Choose only those that you are certain you can perform successfully.

In the art of singing it is especially important to apply everything with taste and in appropriate measure. As a recent example, let me cite the abuse of the device that in French we call *vibration*. Mme. Malibran,[15] that great singer whom we still mourn and whose equal it would be difficult to find, knew how to use this device to great effect. A *vibration*[16] when properly employed can endow a musical phrase with accent and expression, but when it is overused or forced, not only does it result in monotony, but even the freshest voice can quickly become tired.

We come at last to the third phase of my operatic career— that of my entry into the Opéra-Comique. Here I found tasks of a type that was new to me; a new direction was given to a lifetime of study. While at the Théâtre-Italien and at the Opéra I had been the interpreter of Spontini, Meyerbeer, and especially of Rossini, the Italian star, I now was called upon to pop-

ularize the brilliant operas of our celebrated French star, Auber. In a few years I created role upon role in operas that were generally successful; at their head I would place *L'Ambassadrice* and *Le Domino noir.* I also owe a debt to M. Halévy, who has already produced *L'Éclair* and *La Juive,* a work no less remarkable than *Le Shérif.* At the Opéra-Comique the audience was supportive as always, exuding a goodwill that sustained and consoled me even in those theatrical crises that should never have occurred. There too, the orchestra, composed of truly distinguished musicians, welcomed each evening the new embellishments I devised; the last time was in the very recent production of Adolphe Adam's opera, *Rose de Péronne.* It is here that I ended my artistic career.

For the past fifteen years, beginning some time before I left the stage, I have pursued the quite difficult but honorable career of a professor. I intend to follow this career and to end it fittingly after having inspired in you a love for our art.

One more word of advice, my dear students; nowadays, praise is bestowed very freely and has become quite banal. Do not fall prey to its false blandishments; judge yourselves severely before you believe the praise that is bestowed on you by others. There is hardly a beginner that the press will not proclaim to be a colossal talent, no matter how little the actual merit.

Consider: the greatest difficulty facing an artist lies not in acquiring a certain reputation, but in sustaining it. One attains such a result only by making continued progress at all costs, even the day after achieving a new success; not to move forward in one's art is the same as retrogressing. Remind yourselves that, in the art of singing, the notes in themselves are not everything. Without a doubt, if to a sound musical attitude you add a light and flexible voice that enables you to cope with all the difficulties presented in this volume, you will have gained an advantage that will reinforce your talent considerably. Above all, one must, in effect, "speak" when singing: accent, expression, these are the things that should concern you continually; I have said this to you before in the strongest terms, and I dare to say it again.

Keep on studying, then, my dear students; study to ensure your future reputation, and to ensure as well the good fortune that your talent may one day obtain for you. Seek above all the help of great artists. Cherubini, the immortal composer of so many majestic works, and Rossini, the great master, both had the goodness to speak on my behalf in terms that even today feed my self-love as an artist, in the most delicious way. My wish for you is that you will feel the urge to excel, that you will be on guard against rivalry, and that very soon you will give me the great joy of applauding you.

---

[15][Maria Felicità (García) Malibran (1808–1836), famous contralto with a near-soprano range, achieved success in Paris and London and also in New York, where for two years she sang in her father's touring opera company, playing leading roles in *Don Giovanni,* Rossini's *Otello,* and two of Manuel García's own operas. Her Paris debut was at the Théâtre-Italien, in *Semiramide,* in 1828.]

[16]For a precise definition of this important technical device, see the Introduction.

Classic Bel Canto Technique

My remarks will be brief, because I do not subscribe to the opinion that one can develop good singers by means of fancy theories alone. Even the wisest precepts, no matter how well they are put together, will not produce an artist without benefit of practice.

It will therefore be through the use of practical, well-graduated exercises, and the guidance of an expert teacher, that the student will learn to form and connect the tones, and especially to breathe in a way that conserves breath intelligently to the end of a phrase or vocal passage, without any apparent fatigue.

It is not enough to learn how to shade the tone, that is, to swell or diminish it by degrees; it is also necessary, in certain cases, to know how to introduce a vibration, or how to cover the tone, according to the demands of the text. Intelligent pupils, once their musical sensibility is developed, will be able on their own to find the right vocal effects; above all, however, it is important that these effects should be based on true principles, and not just on the singer's fantasy. The art of singing, like other arts, is subject to certain fundamental rules from which one may not stray. I therefore recommend that, aside from breathing and the placement of the voice, you should pay the greatest possible attention to mastering the following exercises, in which every note must be taken boldly, but without harshness.

The exercises should be sung slowly and very *legato,* then nuanced even in scale passages, which should be sung first *forte* and then *piano.* The pupil should also follow up by singing them mentally, thus becoming accustomed to keeping an exact check on what is being done. Above all, it is absolutely necessary that, in chromatic scales, the mind should at every step be aware of what the voice is doing; this is also an infallible way to eventually overcome all the great vocal difficulties.

EXERCISES

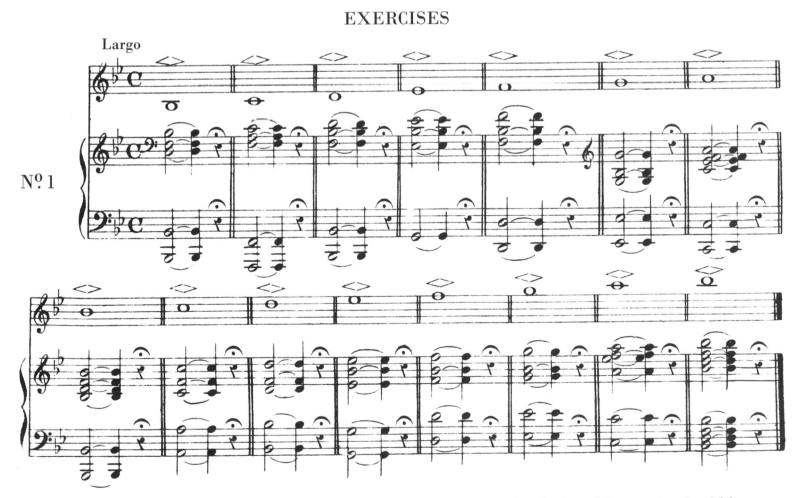

Depending on the student's age and vocal range, the teacher will decide whether this exercise should be sung in B♭ or in C Major.

All the notes should be sung *legato*, and without dragging.

To become accustomed to the leap of an octave, it is always necessary to connect the notes, but those that are marked should be attacked in this manner:

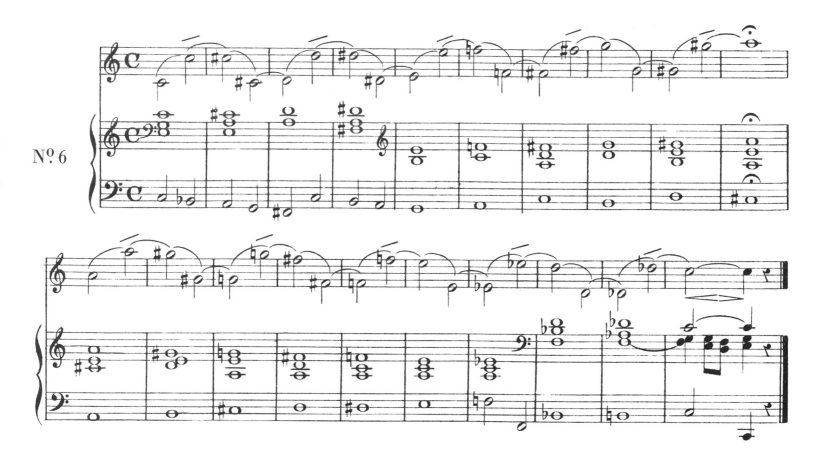

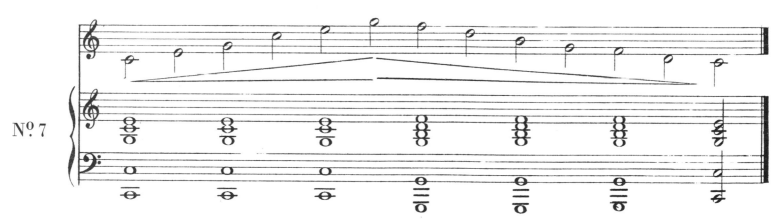

This exercise that we owe to Rossini is the best possible to bring out and develop the voice:

Quicken the tempo a little, and sing the exercise twice as marked, without a breath; the second time, sing it *pianissimo,* with every note sustained and *legato:*

Repeat this exercise in various keys, up to and including the key of F Major.

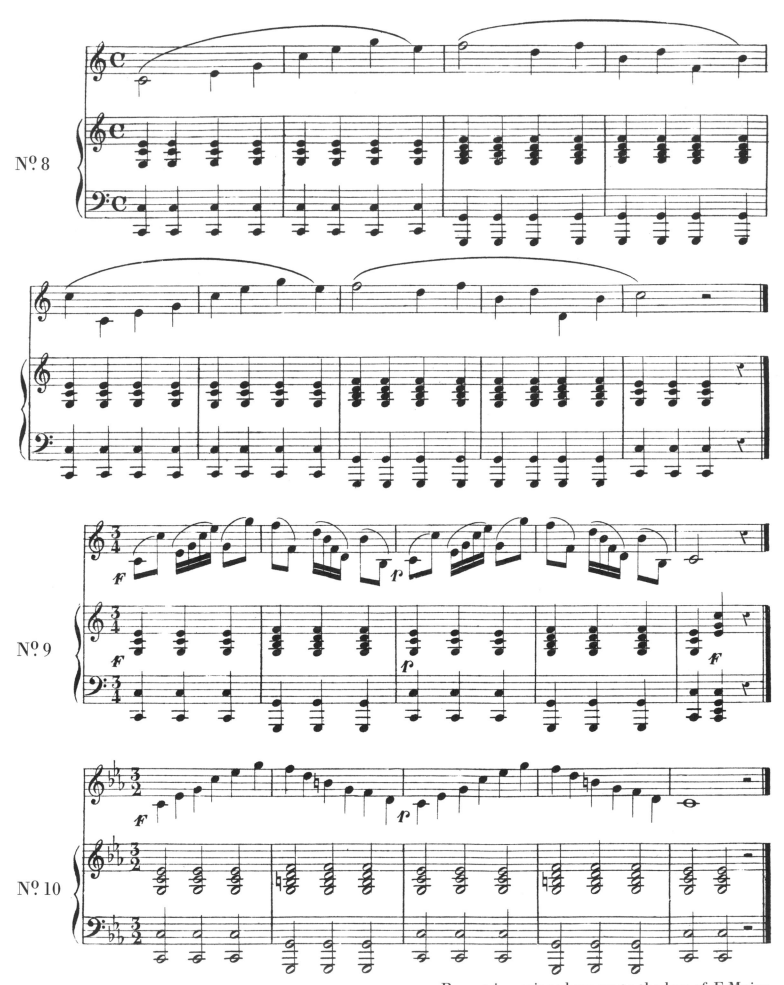

Nº 8

Nº 9

Nº 10

Repeat in various keys up to the key of F Major.

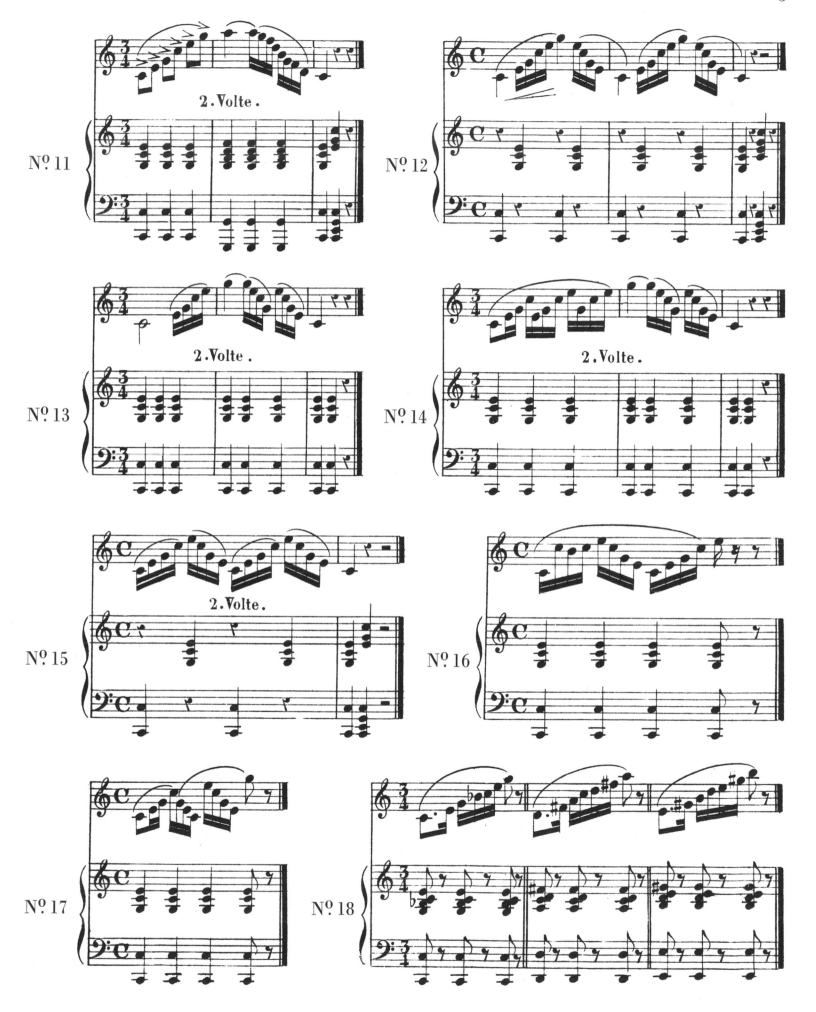

N.º 25

N.º 26

SCALE EXERCISES

Nº 1

Nº 2

Depending on the student's breath control, this exercise should be performed three, four, or five times.

Nº 3

leggero.

As above.

Nº 4

In A Major or in B♭, depending on the student's voice.

Do this exercise on different steps, rising by semitone to B♭ Major.

N.º 6

Do this exercise on different steps.

N.º 7

Observe the nuances as marked.

N.º 8

One frequently finds flexible and agile voices that seem to have no need for all these exercises, but this natural agility is generally detrimental, and often calls for greater study to ensure control than is needed to render it agile. In descending scale passages it is especially important to curb the tendency to sing them too fast, and this can be accomplished by dwelling on some notes, as shown in the following exercise:

For voices that are too agile.

N.º 9

After studying example No. 9 we go on to Nos. 10 and 11, in which one dwells on the note only lightly. The runs should be studied *forte* as well as *piano*.

No. 14

No. 15

In Db, and up by step to the key of F Major.

No. 16

As above.

No. 17

Rising by step to the key of A Major.

Nº 18

Nº 19

Nº 20

14

Nᵒ 21

Nᵒ 22

Up to the key of E Major.

№ 26

№ 27

Do this exercise in B♭,
in B, and in C Major.

Study this slowly at first, and take breath as needed; then strive to sing the first four measures in one breath.

№ 28

Study this as you did the preceding example.

legato

Also study the four measures of Example 28 as they are marked here:

N⁰ 29

Especially with chromatic exercises, it is imperative that they be studied slowly, and that the notes be mentally named as they are sung.

Practice these exercises in different keys.

20

Practice these exercises in different keys.

Nº 38

Nº 39

Nº 40

Nº 41

The turn beginning above the note should be sung very lightly, almost voicelessly, and should come to rest only on the note that follows.

Examples of the turn:

When the turn is from below, accent the first note instead, and diminish the tone immediately.

When a trill does not come naturally, it is necessary to study it from the very first lessons—that is, in the same tempo as the scales. This exercise requires the most painstaking study. One must study it at tempo, as in the following:

EXERCISES FOR THE TRILL

22

After having studied this exercise slowly and in tempo, one should increase the speed and accent the passage as follows:

N.º 2

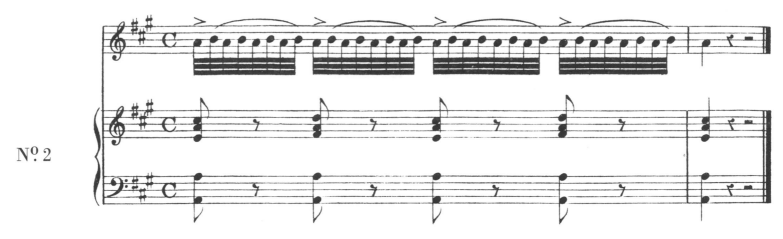

Some students find it easier to begin the trill from above:

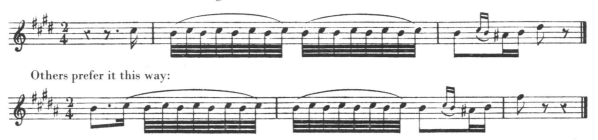

Others prefer it this way:

One should become accustomed to both styles.

STUDY ON THE TRILL

VARIOUS EXERCISES

VARIOUS WAYS OF CONNECTING NOTES

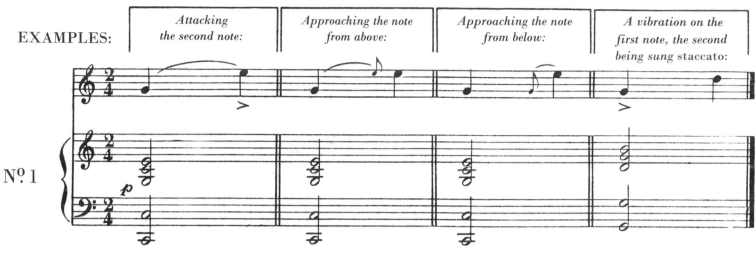

The teacher will point out which particular style is applicable in any given case.

Nº 5

Nº 6

Nº 7

Nº 8

N.º 9

N.º 10

N.º 11

Nº 12

Nº 13

Nº 14

№ 15

№ 16

№ 17

№ 18

Nº 19

Nº 20

Nº 21

Nº 26

Nº 27

Nº 28

Nº 29

leggero

col canto

Nº 30

rall.

No. 31

No. 32

The *staccato* notes are meant to create an effect, but they must not be distorted, nor should they be sung in a dry manner. To avoid this, it is enough to dwell lightly on the preceding note, using a vibration. Example:

NB. Use a vibration on the notes marked

No. 33

They can also be sung without preparation, touching each note lightly, and never harshly. For example:

Practice this exercise up to the key of F Major.

Nº 37

Nº 38

Nº 39

Nº 40

Nº 41

Nº 42

Nº 43

Nº 44

N.º 45

N.º 46

Nº 47

Nº 48

Nº 49

Nº 50

44

EXERCISES FOR THE CADENZAS

TO DEVELOP LIGHTNESS AND ELEGANCE

In general one should reinforce ascending passages:

and make a *diminuendo* when descending:

In general, after having attacked the note on which one finds a fermata, one should sweeten the accentuation of that note so as to impart greater beauty and lightness to the first part of the cadenza. When a voice is spun out in this fashion at the beginning, the passage can easily be finished with greater intensity.

Nº 14

Nº 15

Final cadenzas or embellishments should end with a *rallentando*.

Example:

Nº 16

Nº 17

Nº 18

From this rule one must exempt those cadenzas, at the end of certain pieces, that must be sung with liveliness and *brio*—as in:

Air from **Le Serment**:

Nº 19

tout .... s'ou _ _ bliera

Le Billet de loterie:

Nº 20

Je ne veux pas .... chanter

In the variations in *Les Diamants de la couronne*:

With passages that serve to lead us back to the principal motive, one must tie the motive to the reprise so closely that it becomes an integral part. For example:

In the cavatina in *Semiramide*:

*Marco Aurelio Marliani (1805–1849) studied with Rossini in Paris and became an opera composer.

48

FIRST STUDY
To Place the Voice and Connect Two Notes

SECOND STUDY
On the Turn

THIRD STUDY
On Scale Passages

FOURTH STUDY
On Arpeggios

col canto

a tempo

a tempo

FIFTH STUDY
On Agility

SIXTH STUDY
On Chromatic Passages

FIRST VOCALISE

SECOND VOCALISE

THIRD VOCALISE

FOURTH VOCALISE

FIFTH VOCALISE

SIXTH VOCALISE

Cadenzas, virtuoso passages, and reprises meant to embellish a piece should first of all carry its imprint—that is to say, they should have the same character as the piece and match its tempo. With this end in view, when for example one goes from an *Andante* to an *Allegro* within the same piece, one must take care to change the nature of the embellishments meant for one or the other section. Finally, one must be careful not to mar the composer's intention with ornamentation that is in poor taste. You will find that a serious study of embellishments underlies the fermatas, virtuoso passages, and reprises that follow. It is essential that you scrupulously observe all the nuances that have been called for.

Cadenza for the aria in *Il Giuramento*:

96

Cadenza for the first section of the aria from **Robert le diable,** Act II:

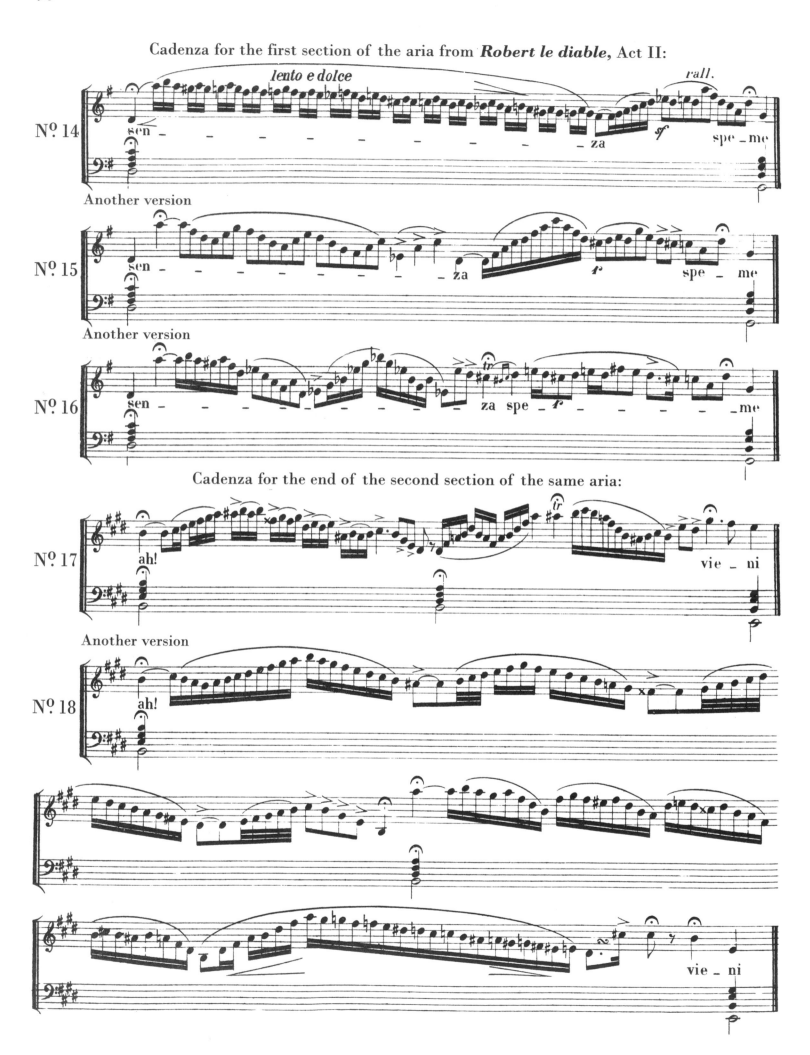

Another version

Another version

Cadenza for the end of the second section of the same aria:

Another version

Virtuoso passage for the aria in **Robert le diable,** Act II:

For the same aria:

Cadenza for Elisabetta's aria from *Le Comte Ory:*

Reprise of the same aria:

Cadenza for the aria in *L'Ambassadrice,* Act I:

Reprise of the same aria:

Another version

From Act I:

From Act I:

Cadenza for the Terzetto in *L'Ambassadrice,* Act II:

In the first section of the aria in Act III:

Cadenza for the aria in Act III:

Virtuoso passage for the repeat of the aria in Act III:

In the same aria:

In the same aria:

Cadenza for the Romanza in *Le Domino noir ("Une fée, un bon ange")*:

Virtuoso passage in the recitative of the aria in *Le Domino noir*, Act III:

Cadenza for the end of the aria:

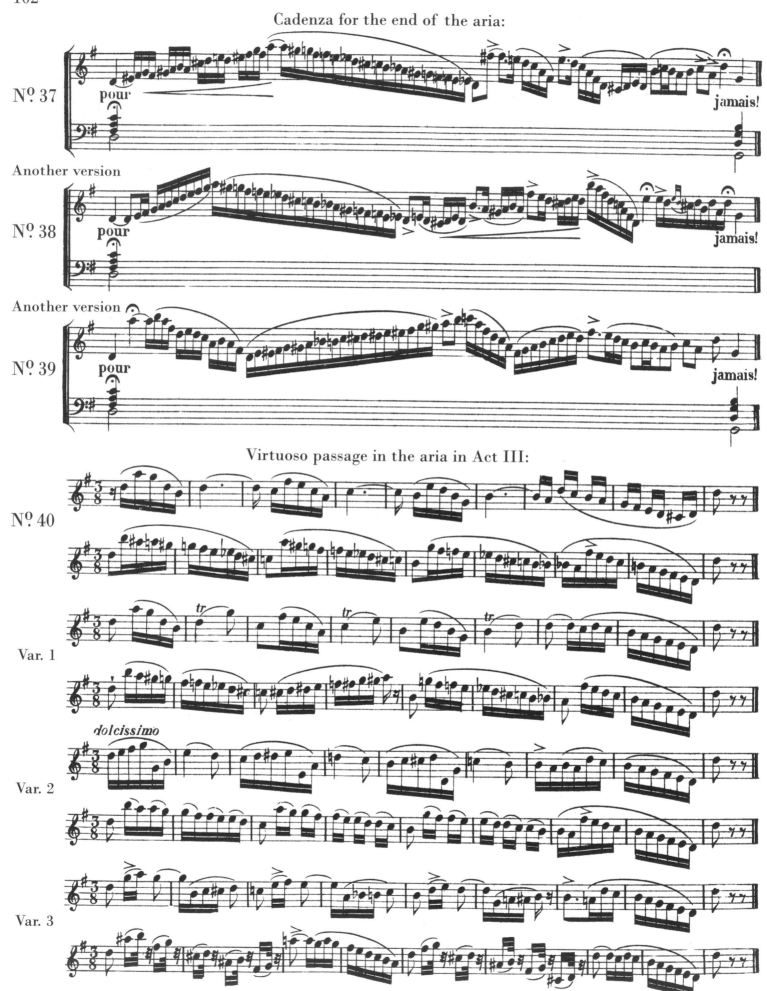

Another version

Another version

Virtuoso passage in the aria in Act III:

For the aria in *Le Shérif*:

For the first section of the duet in *Le Shérif*:

The same duet, second time:

In the aria from *La Rose de Péronne*:

Reprise of the same aria:

In the aria from *Le Philtre:*

In the same aria:

Le Billet de loterie:

Reprise of the same aria:

Nº 49

mais non non non non non non non je ne veux pas chanter

Le Rossignol, with a flute accompaniment provided by M. Tulou*

Nº 50

Chantons en _ sem _ _ _ _ _ _ _ ble   ah..............................

*Jean-Louis Tulou (1786–1865) was "première flute soloist" with the Paris Opéra for thirty years beginning in 1826, and also a professor at the Paris Conservatoire.

APPENDIXES

Operas Mentioned in the Text

Opera Premieres Featuring Mme. Damoreau
(1825–1841)

Operas Mentioned in the Text

By Adolphe Adam (1803–1856)

La Rose de Péronne (The Rose of Peronne)

By Daniel-François Auber (1782–1871)

L'Ambassadrice (The Ambassadress)
Les Diamants de la couronne (The Crown Diamonds)
Le Domino noir (The Black Domino)
La Muette de Portici (The Deaf Woman of Portici)
Le Philtre (The Love Potion)
Le Serment (The Affirmation)

By Vincenzo Bellini (1801–1835)

I Capuletti ed i Montecchi (The Capulets and the Montagues)
La Sonnambula (The Sleepwalker)

By Henri Montan Berton (1767–1844)

Montano et Stéphanie (Montano and Stephanie)

By François-Adrien Boildieu (1775–1834)

Beniowski

By Gaetano Donizetti (1797–1848)

L'Elisir d'amore (The Elixir of Love)

By Manuel del Popolo García (1773–1832)

Il Califfo di Bagdad (The Caliph of Baghdad)

By Jacques-François Halévy (1799–1862)

L'Éclair (The Light)
La Juive (The Jewess)
Le Shérif (The Sheriff)

By Nicolò Isouard (1775–1818)

Le Billet de loterie (The Lottery Ticket)

By Louis Sébastien Lebrun (1764–1829)

Le Rossignol (The Nightingale)

By Vincente Martin y Soler (1754–1806)

Una Cosa rara (A Rare Thing)

By Saverio Mercadante (1795–1870)

Il Giuramento (The Oath)

By Giacomo Meyerbeer (1791–1864)

Robert le diable (Robert the Devil)

By Gioacchino Rossini (1792–1868)

Il Barbiere di Siviglia (The Barber of Seville)
La Cenerentola (Cinderella)
Le Comte Ory (Count Ory)
Guillaume Tell (William Tell)
Semiramide

By Gaspare Spontini (1774–1851)

Fernand Cortez

Opera Premieres
Featuring Mme. Damoreau
(1825–1841)
(in the order of their appearance)

19 June 1825	Contessa di Folleville in Rossini's *Il Viaggio a Reims*. Théâtre des Italiens.
9 October 1826	Pamyre in Rossini's *Le Siège de Corinthe*. Opéra.
26 March 1827	Anai in Rossini's *Moïse et Pharaon*. Opéra.
29 June 1827	Lady Macbeth in Chélard's *Macbeth*. Opéra.
29 February 1828	Elvire in Auber's *La Muette de Portici*. Opéra.
20 August 1828	Adèle in Rossini's *Le Comte Ory*. Opéra.
3 August 1829	Mathilde in Rossini's *Guillaume Tell*. Opéra.
13 October 1830	Ninka in Auber's *Le Dieu et la bayadère*. Opéra.
20 June 1831	Terezine in Auber's *Le Philtre*. Opéra.
21 November 1831	Isabelle in Meyerbeer's *Robert le diable*. Opéra.
1 October 1832	Marie in Auber's *Le Serment*. Opéra.
22 July 1833	Delia in Cherubini's *Ali-Baba*. Opéra.
23 January 1836	Lucrezia in Auber's *Actéon*. Opéra-Comique.
30 June 1836	Unknown role in Monpou's *Le Luthier de Vienne*. Opéra-Comique.
1 October 1836	Unknown role in Puget's *Le Mauvais œil*. Opéra-Comique.
21 December 1836	Henriette in Auber's *L'Ambassadrice*. Opéra-Comique.
1837 [date unknown]	Elaisa in Mercadante's *Il Giuramento*. Théâtre Favart.
2 December 1837	Angèle in Auber's *Le Domino noir*. Opéra-Comique.
2 September 1839	Camilla in Halévy's *Le Shérif*. Opéra-Comique.
18 May 1840	Title role in Auber's *Zanetta*. Opéra-Comique.
12 December 1840	Unknown role in Adam's *La Rose de Péronne*. Opéra-Comique.
6 March 1841	Catarina in Auber's *Les Diamants de la couronne*. Opéra-Comique.
24 December 1849	Unknown role in Adam's *Le Fanal*. Opéra.
	[possibly called out of retirement for this performance]

END OF EDITION